When Sinners Say

"*I Do*"

The Study Guide

DAVE HARVEY

with ERIN SUTHERLAND *and* ANDY FARMER

Shepherd Press
Wapwallopen, Pennsylvania

Contents

Contents

Introduction

This study guide is designed to help you think about and apply the material in *When Sinners Say "I Do."* As I mentioned in the preface of the book, you might be curious about a guy who would write a book titled, *When Sinners Say "I Do."* My name is Dave and . . . well . . . I'm a sinner. Saying "I do" twenty-five years ago to my beautiful wife not only didn't solve that problem, it magnified it times ten. Engaged people can sometimes wonder whether "I do" holds a magical power that charms us into selfless and instinctively caring people. It doesn't. Would I have said, "I do" if I knew what "I do" really meant? Without a doubt. Would the grin in my wedding pictures have been less self-confident and more, how shall I say it, *desperate*? Most assuredly!

What do I mean when I say I'm a sinner? Picture in your mind a guy in sackcloth and ashes, prostrate on the ground, throwing dust on his head in shame.

No, scratch that. Picture this instead.

I used to have a fail-safe system for vacuuming my car. Give me fifty cents and four minutes, and you could do surgery on my carpets. The key is mat placement, nimble feet, and doors ajar. Once the machine sprang to life, I would work like a human black hole, sucking everything into the vacuum that wasn't bolted down. Sure there was a cost—I lost important papers, checks and even a pet or two—but there are always casualties in the maintenance of an orderly system. It was my way. The only way.

Have you ever been so devoted to your way that it makes you, well . . . stupid?

I found a passage from the Bible that describes the biggest problem for me and the biggest challenge in my marriage. "For the desires of the flesh are against the Spirit, and the desires of the Spirit are against the flesh, for these are opposed to each other, to keep you from doing the things you want to do" (Galatians 5:17).

What I love about this passage is not just that it describes my life so well; it's that it was written by somebody who you assume would have solved the sin problems of life. Isn't Paul the one who wrote, "I can do all things through him who strengthens me" (Philippians 4:13). True, but he's also the guy who confessed, "Wretched man that I am! Who will deliver me from this body of death?" (Romans 7:24). The Apostle Paul was wretched? How does that work? Man, he must have been really bad. But what if I told you that a great marriage—a God-glorifying, soul-inspiring, life-enduring union—springs from the conviction that we are sinners just like Paul. Would that intrigue you enough to go to the next chapter? That's where we are headed, if you have the courage to come. Curious?

To say "I am a sinner" is to stare boldly at a fundamental reality that many people don't even want to glance at. But when we acknowledge that painful reality in our lives, several great things become clear. The greatest benefit of acknowledging our sinfulness is that it makes Christ and his work precious to us. Like Jesus said, "Those who are well have no need for a physician, but those who are sick. I have not come to call the righteous but sinners to repentance" (Luke 5:31–32). Only sinners need a Savior.

That's the beginning that leads us to grace. This is not a depressing thought. It recognizes that to get to the heart of marriage, we must deal with the heart of sin. A great pastor once said, "Till sin be bitter, Christ will not be sweet." He was getting at a profound truth of the gospel. Until we understand the problem, we will not be able to delight in the solution. Grace is truly amazing because of what we're saved from. There lies hope for sinners who say "I do."

Part of learning about that grace is applying it to our marriages. This study guide is formatted in a way to help with personal application, conversation as a couple, and for small group discussion as well. We've included a one page summary of key points from the chapter so you can quickly remember the basic points in the book. The questions are designed to help individuals, couples and small groups wrestle with and apply the themes in the book to their own lives. There are different types of questions included: we call them Gospel Application and Gospel Interaction questions because we want to make sure the gospel is never far from our mind in either personal application or group discussion.

Gospel Application Questions

For Me Questions: these are questions designed to help an individual reader apply the book on a personal level.

For Us Questions: these are questions that a couple can talk about together.

Gospel Interaction Questions

Small Group Questions: these are designed for a small group to stimulate further conversation. If you are leading the discussion, you can also bring in the Gospel Application questions as appropriate for use in your group.

My prayer is that as you work through this study guide, you will freshly experience the grace our Savior has for each of us. Before going any further, can I urge you to pray? Pray that God would help you and your spouse. Pray that God would give you much grace to see how his gospel is at work in your marriage and how his grace is at work to change you. Pray that he would provide his Holy Spirit to help you apply the truths of Scripture. May you find his blessing abundant!

Chapter One

What Really Matters In Marriage

Gospel Implication

Have you ever buttoned your shirt wrong . . . you know, so the holes and buttons don't match up and the shirt looks like it was pasted on by first-graders? (Just a hunch, but this is probably a guy thing.) It recently happened to me. I got the first button in the wrong hole and kept going until I was sporting a fashion nightmare. Funny thing was, I thought I looked great—maybe I had an extra button at the bottom, but that was obviously a defect in the shirt.

Moments like this put my wife, Kimm, in an awkward position. *Should I fix him again?* she ponders, *or just allow the guys at the office to enjoy it?* This time she was merciful, and I had a properly-buttoned day. It's amazing how distorted and disheveled one can look from not getting that first button right. Start off in the wrong place, and there's no way to correct the problem down the line. Getting the first one right is the key to getting everything else right.

Marriage is like that shirt. If you get the first things right, then the many other "buttons" of marriage—communication, conflict resolution, romance, roles—all start to line up in a way that works together.

Key Idea: *What we believe about God determines the quality of our marriage.*

In this chapter, we learn that we are all theologians—we all think about God. Let me take a moment to explain. Everybody views life from a perspective—what some call a worldview. Our worldview is shaped by many things: our culture, our gender, our upbringing, our present situation, etc. The most profound thing that shapes anybody's worldview is their understanding of God. What a person believes about God determines what he or she thinks about how we got here, what our ultimate meaning is, and what happens after we die. So essentially our worldview, our perspective on life, is determined by our perspective on God. And when we talk about theology, all we are talking about is what we think about God. What you truly believe about God and what it means to live for God *is* your theology.

What kind of theologian are you? It's not hard to tell. Whether we realize it or not, our ideas about life, needs, marriage, romance, conflict, and everything else reveal themselves all the time in our words and deeds, inevitably reflecting our view of God. If you listen closely, theology spills from our lips everyday.

The gospel is an endless fountain of God's grace in your marriage. To become a good theologian and to be able to look forward to a lifelong, thriving marriage, you must have a clear understanding of the gospel. Without it, you *cannot* see God, yourself, or your marriage for what they truly are. The gospel is the fountain of a thriving marriage.

Gospel Application

For Me:

1. What is the gospel?

   Take a few minutes to write it down in one paragraph as simply as possible; keep the paragraph handy so that you can look at it often through this study to remind yourself of the ultimate purpose of marriage.

2. Think about an ordinary experience from your marriage this week—a change in plans, a conflict, an unexpected surprise. How did you handle that experience (in words and deeds)? And what did that event reveal about your view of God in that moment?

3. In your own words, write out your goal for your marriage.

For Us:

1. How does the gospel give us hope in our marriage?

2. In what ways is our marriage on a solid biblical foundation? In what ways does our marriage need to change in order to align more fully with biblical teaching? Consider how you might work on those areas.

3. What is one way I can grow in helping you to experience the gospel in our marriage?

4. Write down one of the areas where you're aware of needing to grow in your marriage; also write down where you most struggle to trust God in these areas. What promises does God make in Scripture that you can meditate on to grow in bringing the gospel to bear in your marriage in these areas?

Gospel Interaction—
Small Group Discussion

1. If you have worked on the *Gospel Application* questions above, share some of your answers with your small group.

2. How has your marriage become sweeter since you first said "I do"?

3. Think back to your wedding day. How would you have answered the question: "How do you know this marriage is going to work?" Do you identify with any of the answers going through the minds of the congregation at the wedding example on pp. 18–19?

4. Why is a robust view of sin helpful to marriage?

5. What is one present area you would like to see improve in your marriage?

6. As you begin to look at your marriage in light of chapter 1:

   • Where are you more aware of God's grace and mercy in your spouse?

   • What do you think will be most challenging for you personally as you continue reading this book?

Responses:

Gospel Reflection

QUOTE: *"What comes into our minds when we think about God, is the most important thing about us."*

—A.W. Tozer, p. 31

SCRIPTURE: EPHESIANS 3:14–20

Notes:

Chapter Two

Waking Up With
the Worst of Sinners

Gospel Implication

*T*he opening of chapter 2 details an illustration of how I can so quickly react to situations that aren't quite to my liking. This is how it happens: Kimm is running late; I get angry and tell her. Despite my sinful reaction in this situation, Kimm is once again able to cover my words over with love and patience and help me to see what is wrong with them. I'm so grateful for Kimm's help, but at that time, the question is lingering: if I love my wife, why do I find it so easy to treat her like I don't?

This is the underside of marriage, the reality of living with someone day to day in a fallen world. Paul wrote to Timothy, "The saying is trustworthy and deserving of full acceptance, that Christ Jesus came into the world to save sinners, of whom I am the foremost" (1 Timothy 1:15). In effect, Paul is saying,

"Look, I know my sin. And what I've seen in my own heart is darker and more awful; it's more proud, selfish and self-exalting; and it's more consistently and regularly in rebellion against God than anything I have seen." But, Paul doesn't stop there. His acute awareness of his sinful state leads him to magnify the glory of the Savior!

Back to my illustration, it was my sin. And this sin—my sin and yours—is supremely ugly. It is vile. It is wicked. But at the same time it is the backdrop to a larger drama. We may be works in progress who are painfully prone to sin, yet we can be joyful works, for—thanks be to God—we have been redeemed by grace through the death and resurrection of Christ. Our Savior has come to rescue us from the penalty of sin and grant us an abundant life by his Spirit. As two people in marriage embrace this view of reality, and live in accordance with it, their lives and marriage begin to look more and more like the picture God wants to display to a lost world. Until sin be bitter, marriage may not be sweet.

This ongoing need for the Savior is exactly what professing Christians must hang on to. The cross makes a stunning statement about husbands and wives: we are sinners and our only hope is grace. Without a clear awareness of sin, we will evaluate our conflicts outside of the biblical story—the finished work of Jesus Christ on the cross—thus eliminating any basis for true understanding, true reconciliation, or true change. Without the gospel of our crucified and risen Savior our marriages slide toward the superficial. We begin to make limp justifications for our sinful behavior, and our marriage conflicts end, at best, in uneasy, partial, negotiated settlements.

But once I find 1 Timothy 1:15–16 trustworthy—once I can embrace it with full acceptance—once I know that I am indeed the worst of sinners, then my spouse is no longer my biggest problem: *I am.* And when I find myself walking in the shoes of the worst of sinners, I will make every effort to grant my spouse the same lavish grace that God has granted me. The question that used to boggle my mind, "*If I love my wife, why do I find it so easy to treat her like I don't?*" has a universal answer. We are all the worst of sinners, so anything we do that *isn't* sin is simply the grace of God at work.

Key Idea: *Until sin be bitter, marriage may not be sweet.*

Gospel Application

For Me:

1. Read 1 Timothy 1:15–17; how have you experienced the mercy of God in the face of your sin over the last week?

2. Consider the question that so easily boggled my mind: *If I love my [spouse], why do I find it so easy to treat [him or her] like I don't?* How does the universal answer (a sinner forgiven by grace) to that question affect the way you view your spouse?

3. Which of the following phrases might best describe how you view yourself:

   • Innocent till proven guilty
   • Worse than some, better than others
   • Good days/bad days
   • I'm doing the best I can
   • I'm the worst of sinners

4. How might your answer to this question affect your approach to God? What about to your marriage?

For Us:

1. Talk with your spouse about ways that God is currently at work. What is one way you've seen your spouse grow in the last month?

2. Write down some words that currently define the way you relate to your spouse. How would these words change if you made it your goal to live with your spouse as if you are the worst of sinners? Write down what changes you would anticipate and discuss them with your spouse.

3. Ask your spouse the following: "After you've read Owen's definition of humility on p. 44, are there specific areas where I can grow in how I define humility?"

Gospel Interaction—
Small Group Discussion

1. If you have worked on the *Gospel Application* questions above, share some of your answers with your small group.

2. What in this chapter do you find helpful towards understanding the daily battles in your marriage (like the opening illustration)?

3. What does it mean to think of yourself as the "worst of sinners?" Why do you think it's important to see sin as the worst problem we face in marriage?

4. How does the gospel keep us from fueling condemnation when we acknowledge that we are the worst of sinners?

5. Look through Rob and Sally's story (pp. 39–41). Are there things in this story that are familiar to you? How would you try to help them?

Responses:

Gospel Reflection

QUOTE: *"Sin is wrong, not because of what it does to me, or my spouse, or child, or neighbor, but because it is an act of rebellion against the infinitely majestic God."*

—Jerry Bridges, p. 42

SCRIPTURE: PSALM 40

Notes:

Chapter Three

The Fog of War
and the Law of Sin

Gospel Implication

*I*n this chapter and the next, we want to understand this thing called sin a little better, examining its nature and learning how we tend to respond to it. After all, when you're the worst of sinners, it pays to know a few things about how sin actually works.

I started this chapter with the story of a battle—the Battle of Bull Run. It was the first major battle of the Civil War on July 21, 1861. The roar of artillery seemed to awaken all of Virginia as the Union and Confederate armies clashed among the farms by the stream called Bull Run. As the battle intensified, a strange thing occurred. Hundreds of Washingtonians—Senators, Representatives, government workers and their families, all dressed in leisure apparel and carrying picnic baskets—raced to the hill to watch the battle unfold. Armed with opera glasses to survey the fighting, they chatted amicably as men were slaughtered on the fields below. As spirits were high and entertainment level maximized, a Rebel counterattack occurred, sweeping over the Union flank. This put the army to flight and the implications became obvious. The serene picnic ground was about to become a battle zone. Mass confusion erupted as the spectators fled, just moments before the Confederate wave washed over the hill. The entertainment was over. The battle was upon them.

A battle, like the Battle of Bull Run, represents the nature of sin. You see, sin is war. Sin creates war—war with God, war with others, and war within yourself. Now, in marriage what do you have —two sinners, each with the potential for war constantly lurking within them. Marriage, after all, is just life in a particularly concentrated form. Is it any wonder, then, that just as war overran the shocked and clueless picnickers at the Battle of Bull Run, the war of sin can sometimes engulf us when we least expect it?

In Scripture, James 4:1–3 explains what we experience:

"What causes quarrels and what causes fights among you? Is it not this, that your passions are at war within you? You desire and do not have, so you murder. You covet and cannot obtain, so you fight and quarrel. You do not have, because you do not ask. You ask and do not receive, because you ask wrongly, to spend it on your passions."

Sin is crafty. Sin is alluring. Sin betrays us. We *must* fight the battle with sin. If we don't, it *will* overrun us. As we battle, though we must not forget that we stand *forgiven in God's court* because of the atoning sacrifice of Christ—God no longer views us in relationship to our sin (Romans 8:1–4). And we are welcomed as *righteous in God's house* because of the imputed righteousness of Christ! God sees you as more than a forgiven sinner. He sees you as a holy person. Even though the power of sin continues to operate within you, its reign has been broken and God no longer sees you in reference to it.

Key Idea: *No matter how intense your battle with sin may rage, you fight as a forgiven sinner. You fight on the side of God, and God always wins in the end!*

As we fight this battle within, and help our spouse to fight, we have confidence that one day it will end, and the peace, which right now guards us in Christ, will be ours fully and for eternity.

Gospel Application

For Me:

1. How does Galatians 2:19–21 provide hope for you?

2. Write out one area where you can experience fatigue in the battle against sin. What is one promise God specifically provides in His Word that can help to strengthen you in the battle in these areas?

3. Read Romans 8:1–4 (printed on page 57). How does this passage speak to the worst of sinners—you and your spouse?

For Us:

1. One way I see God's grace at work in you, helping you to fight the battle of sin as a *forgiven sinner* is . . .

2. What is one way you see the 'law of sin' at work in my life?

3. What are some common things that generate conflict in our marriage? How do they compare to what James 4:1–3 (printed on page 51) says about the cause of conflict?

Gospel Interaction—
Small Group Discussion

1. If you have worked on the *Gospel Application* questions above, share some of your answers with your small group.

2. How should the truth that we already have victory in Christ over our sin affect our approach to battling sin?

3. Do you remember the last time you experienced a "soul skirmish" or "the battle within"? List some words that describe the way that battle felt.

4. Discuss the implications of these two truths: *we stand forgiven in God's court* and *we are welcomed as righteous in God's house.* How should those truths affect your life? Your spouse? Your marriage?

5. On pp. 49–50 there are some examples of how the battle within can play out for a husband and wife in marriage. Can you think of your own experiences that might be similar to what is described on these pages?

6. Why might it be so difficult to see how grace is at work in our conflicts?

Responses:

Gospel Reflection

QUOTE: *"In one sense, life doesn't begin to get complicated until one becomes a Christian. When we are born of the Spirit we are born anew into a fierce struggle between the old man and the new man."*

—R.C. Sproul, p. 53

SCRIPTURE: ROMANS 7:22–23

Notes:

Chapter Four

Taking It Out for a Spin

Gospel Implication

*R*esponding to the truths we've learned about the nature of sin requires two things: (1) grace—and a lot of it and (2) hard work. I open this chapter with an illustration from my childhood when my friend, Terry, and I sat in his brother's souped up Chrysler, revving the engine. Terry was perched behind the wheel, punching the accelerator to the excitement of the crowd of teenage boys who had gathered to watch. As the co-pilot, I began to wonder what the point of gunning the engine was if we weren't going anywhere? I should have left it a question, but instead, my hand slowly reached for the gearshift. Terry was oblivious. As he waved to the growing group of kids, I jerked the gearshift into drive just as the accelerator was pushed. We learned that this Chrysler had pick-up! Fortunately, no damage was done.

What compels two teenage kids to act in such an audacious manner? Teenagers don't want to sit still. They want to put life in gear. And there's something of that restless desire in our relationship with God. God's grace at work in us compels us to not just sit behind the steering wheel, but put what we know into gear. When God saves us, we are drawn to unfamiliar things—to holiness, truth, the Scriptures, and God's amazing love. As we learn more, though, we have a desire to act on what we know and believe about God.

Key Idea: *God's grace at work in us compels us to not just sit behind the steering wheel, but to put what we know into gear.*

In this chapter, we look at how progress comes when we slip our theology into gear and find out what it can do. Though more extensively explained in chapter 4 of the book, here's a brief summary of the four gears you can engage.

First Gear: In Humility, Suspect Yourself First

It is very important in our Christian lives to be suspicious of any claims to righteousness we bring to our relationship with God. It is in Christ alone, and in his merit alone, that we trust. True humility is living confident in Christ's righteousness, and suspicious of our own.

Second Gear: In Integrity, Inspect Yourself

Most clearly stated in Matthew 7:3–5, we see that we need to slow down and inspect our own heart first:

How can you say to your brother, "Let me take the speck out of your eye," when there is the log in your own eye? You hypocrite, first take the log out of your own eye, and then you will see clearly to take the speck out of your brother's eye.

In using the image of logs and specks, Jesus reveals this approach as wrong, ineffective (to put it mildly), and absurd.

When our goal is to address someone else's sin, Jesus tells us, *our own sin* must loom large in our sight. It must be, by far, the primary and more significant issue. Jesus is not concerned here with which of you is *more at fault* in a particular instance. His emphasis is your *focus*, what you find to be the *most obvious fact* to you whenever sin is in view. He's calling for the inspection to begin with me.

Third Gear: Admit that Circumstances Only Reveal Existing Sin

As we have already learned, our problems come from how our hearts engage with the circumstances around us. If we are applying gospel wisdom, we see the hand of God in every situation, working for our ultimate good. In marriage, this means that God will create opportunities to reveal and then deal with sin that keeps us from living in wisdom.

You see, your wicked heart and mine are amazingly similar. They both crave vindication. They want to insist that something else made us sin . . . something outside of us . . . beyond our control. Aha—our circumstances!

Fourth Gear: Focus on Undeserved Grace, Not Unmet Needs

Needs are not wrong; we all have them. They exist as daily reminders that we were created as dependent beings in fundamental need of God and his provision for our lives. But maintaining a distinction between genuine needs and those needs invented by a self-indulgent culture is essential for a healthy marriage.

Gospel Application

For Me:

1. Where does God's grace seem to be compelling you to put what you know into gear?

2. Rate yourself from one to ten on self-suspicion. One is "I assume whatever the problem, it isn't with me." Ten is "I assume whatever the problem, I am the cause." In light of what you've read, where do you think you should be?

3. How does a biblical self-understanding help us in resolving conflict with our spouse?

For Us:

1. Take time to think about and write out how God's grace is currently active in your marriage. Discuss these with your spouse.

2. Discuss your most recent conflict. Ask your spouse whether they felt like you related to them as a project to be fixed more than a partner in grace. Take time to pray and thank God for his grace to reconcile the conflict. Ask for fresh grace to live more suspicious of self than your spouse.

Gospel Interaction—
Small Group Discussion

1. If you have worked on the *Gospel Application* questions above, share some of your answers with your small group.

2. What are some ways that God has captivated you with his grace over the last week?

3. Why is being self-suspicious a good thing?

4. Which of the four gears listed in this chapter do you find it easiest to drive in marriage these days? Most difficult?

5. Is there any time you tried to "fix" your spouse? What happened?

6. What are some things about you that would tend to tempt your spouse to sin, specifically to be angry?

7. How would you respond to someone indicating they are experiencing irreconcilable differences with their spouse?

Responses:

Gospel Reflection

QUOTE: *"Our best works are shot through with sin and contain something for which we need to be forgiven."*

—J.I. Packer p. 65

SCRIPTURE: JAMES 4:1–3

Notes:

Chapter Five

Mercy Triumphs
over Judgment

Gospel Implication

*M*ercy is a unique, marvelous, exceptional word. God's mercy means his kindness, patience, and forgiveness toward us. It is his compassionate willingness to suffer for and with sinners for their ultimate good.

In the Bible, mercy weds the severe obligation of justice with the warmth of personal relationship. Mercy explains how a holy and loving God can relate to sinners without compromising who he is. God doesn't thump his chest and parade this attribute, as if it's unique to him but unattainable by us. He gives it to us freely, a gift to pass along. "Be merciful, even as your Father is merciful" (Luke 6:36).

Do you know God as a God of mercy? Do you see your spouse as God sees him or her—through eyes of mercy? If your answer to either question is no, it is unlikely that your marriage is sweet. Mercy sweetens marriage. Where it is absent, two people flog one another over everything from failure to fix the faucet to phone bills. But where it is present, marriage grows sweeter and more delightful, even in the face of challenges, setbacks, and the persistent effects of our remaining sin.

Mercy doesn't change the need to speak truth. It transforms our motivation from a desire to win battles to a desire to represent Christ. It takes me out of the center and puts Christ in the center. It sweetens all it touches because it comes from heaven—from the very throne of the merciful Savior. Mercy is a blessing to those who receive and those who give.

Key Idea: *Mercy sweetens marriage and it is given.*

Gospel Application

For Me:

1. What did you learn about mercy in this chapter? What does it mean to you that God is merciful?

2. Think about an experience where you received mercy from someone else. What is the effect of those experiences on your life?

For Us:

1. In considering how to "do unto others," complete the following statement and share it with your spouse:

   One thing about the gospel that best helps me to not respond sinfully toward you in a situation is . . .

2. What are some practical ways you express kindness in your marriage?

Gospel Interaction—
Small Group Discussion

1. If you have worked on the *Gospel Application* questions above, share some of your answers with your small group.

2. Describe a way you have seen mercy expressed in your marriage.

3. What are some ways you can express kindness in your marriage?

4. Which of the courtroom questions on pp. 91–92 would be most helpful for you to ask yourself when you feel wronged?

5. What does Gordon and Emma's story say about God's goal for marriage?

6. Are there any situations you can think of where we shouldn't be merciful? (Before you answer, reread the parable in Luke 6:27–36 and the comments on p. 83.)

Responses:

Gospel Reflection

QUOTES:
"The quality of mercy is not strain'd,
It droppeth as the gentle rain from heaven
Upon the place beneath. It is twice blest:
It blesseth him that gives and him that takes."

—Shakespeare, p. 96

"God's power operates best in human weakness.
Weakness is the arena in which God can most effec-
tively manifest his power."

—John Stott, p. 93

SCRIPTURE: LUKE 6: 36

Notes:

Chapter Six

Forgiveness, Full and Free

Gospel Implication

 he agreement was to write off forty billon dollars of debt, an unprecedented move in international relations. The nations represented at the 2005 G8 Summit had decided to cancel the debt of the eighteen highly indebted poor countries in Africa who qualified for debt reduction. It was the largest debt cancellation in history. The G8's action testified to the member nations' ability to benevolently overlook mere economic interests. Forty billion dollars—that's a lot of zeros! As the reports confirming this dramatic generosity raced around the globe, one thing became clear: canceling an enormous debt makes an enormous statement.

In the previous chapter we discussed the power of mercy in marriage—how the call to mercy comes from the mercy we've received from God in Christ. In this chapter we look at another aspect of mercy: forgiveness.

In Scripture, the ideas of mercy and forgiveness are so intertwined as to be almost synonymous. But there is an important difference. Mercy can be extended to those who don't recognize it, whereas forgiveness is most often a transaction between parties.

True forgiveness sees another's sin for the evil that it is, addresses it, then absorbs the cost of that sin by the power of God's abundant grace. Such forgiveness sets the sinner free; the account of the sin is closed, canceled, blotted out. There is nothing in us that would naturally choose the way of full, biblical forgiveness. It's just too hard, and adding to the challenge is the fact that the extension of true forgiveness can never guarantee we won't be wronged again. So why even consider it? Because forgiveness, full and free, is precisely what has been accomplished for us on Calvary. And the one who has been forgiven is now able to forgive others.

Key Idea: *Forgiven sinners forgive sin (Matthew 18:23–35).*

Gospel Application

For Me:

1. Describe how you understood forgiveness before reading this chapter. What have you learned about forgiveness that you didn't consider before?

2. List two specific sins that you know God has forgiven you of through the atonement of his Son on the cross.

   • On the cross Jesus brought particular forgiveness from God to me for . . .
   • On the cross Jesus brought particular forgiveness from God to me for . . .

For Us:

1. In light of this chapter, discuss how well you resolve conflict through forgiveness in your marriage.

2. Ask each other: are you aware of any possible judgmental attitudes that I have had toward you that I need to reconsider in light of the forgiveness of God for my sin against Him?

3. Pray together and ask God to help you continue to forgive each other.

Gospel Interaction—
Small Group Discussion

1. If you have worked on the *Gospel Application* questions above, share some of your answers with your small group.

2. Share the story of God's forgiveness to you—how he saved you and extended his forgiveness to you.

3. What does it mean that "the status of the one sinned against is the key" to understanding forgiveness (p. 103)?

4. Read about the three valves for the process of forgiveness on pages 106–107. Which of these three valves do you find most difficult to open?

5. Consider the story of Jeremy and Cindy in this chapter. Though you may have never experienced the reality of adultery in your marriage, is there anything they thought, said or did that you can identify with at some point in your marriage? Underline it and consider sharing it in fellowship with others.

6. Think about the little 100 denarii things you do against your spouse. Are any of the following rationalizations familiar to you?

- I didn't mean it
- Don't be so sensitive
- You deserved it
- You do it too
- It's just a misunderstanding
- I'm just having a bad day
- (Your own particular favorite)

Why don't these comments make as much sense to your spouse when they hear them as they do to you when you say them?

Responses:

Gospel Reflection

QUOTE: *"Forgiveness can be a costly activity. When you cancel a debt, it does not just simply disappear. Instead, you absorb a liability that someone else deserves to pay. Similarly, forgiveness requires that you absorb certain effects of another person's sins and you release that person from liability to punishment. This is precisely what Christ accomplished on Calvary."*

—Ken Sande, p. 108

SCRIPTURE: MATTHEW 18:21–35

Notes:

Chapter Seven

The Surgeon, the Scalpel, and the Spouse in Sin

Gospel Implication

This chapter begins by describing the scene of 2 Samuel—a story of adultery, deception, and murder made all the more shocking because it was committed by the greatest and most honorable king in the entire history of Israel. David was a man after God's own heart (1 Samuel 13:14). But he took extraordinary risks to indulge himself and then disguise his adultery. While his plans to exonerate himself from the consequences of his sin seemed to go smoothly, David discovered later that all he cherished was on a collision course with God's justice. Ascending the palace steps was his old friend, the prophet Nathan. This wasn't a social call. It was a rescue mission.

Nathan stood before a man he loved but hardly recognized, a king deceived and drifting perilously toward destruction.

The prophet took no joy in the sharp words forming in his mind. He had no way to predict how David would respond to his rebuke. But when someone close to you is running from the truth, love demands that you speak. Sometimes love must risk peace for the sake of truth. David was about to be loved in one of the hardest possible ways. And he didn't even have to leave the house.

There are two amazing dynamics at work in this historical snapshot. First, God pursues sinners. God's love is relentless. Even when we are blinded by sin, he refuses to let go. God pursued David with a tireless love. Second, God uses sinners to pursue sinners. Nathan, like David, was a man prone to the same temptations and failures as David. But God had given Nathan a ministry in that moment. He was a sinner called to help another sinner become reconciled to God.

Matthew Henry once said, "The three qualifications of a good surgeon are requisite in a reprover: He should have an eagle's eye, a lion's heart, and a lady's hand; in short, he should be endued with wisdom, courage, and meekness."

This great Puritan had struck upon a wonderful metaphor. Reproof—the means by which a Nathan reaches into the soul of one trapped in sin to bring the ministry of reconciliation—is a lot like surgery. Both require care, wisdom, and precision, as well as a delicate and determined hand.

Key Idea: *A good surgeon displays wisdom, courage and meekness.*

Gospel Application

For Me:

1. List some "evidences of grace" (p. 132) over the past week from your own life and that of your spouse. Share them with your spouse.

2. Take time to consider and answer the 'diagnostic pre-op' questions on pages 124–126. Which of those truths do you need to most often remind yourself?

For Us:

1. Ask your spouse: "How can I grow in the surgical skill of meekness as described in this chapter?"

2. Each of you complete this sentence: If you are going to be a helpful Nathan who helps me receive correction, you could . . .

Gospel Interaction—
Small Group Discussion

1. If you have worked on the *Gospel Application* questions above, share some of your answers with your small group.

2. Have you ever found yourself in a Nathan-like situation, needing to go to someone to confront them on something they have done? What are some thoughts and feelings you have experienced in that situation?

3. What kinds of character qualities does it take to be a good Nathan in your marriage?

4. What does this chapter say about repentance (pp. 127–129) that may be new to your thinking?

5. To be a good spiritual surgeon to our spouse, we need three spiritual skills—wisdom, meekness and courage. If you had to go to spiritual surgery school, how would you arrange your three skill classes for what you need most? Explain why you would arrange them that way.

Responses:

Gospel Reflection

QUOTE: *"Identify evidences of grace in others. This means actively looking for ways that God is at work in the lives of other people."*

—C.J. Mahaney, p. 132

SCRIPTURE: PSALM 51

Notes:

Chapter Eight

Stubborn Grace

Gospel Implication

A great theologian of our time, J. I. Packer, has observed, "No need in Christendom is more urgent than the need for a renewed awareness of what the grace of God really is." I couldn't agree more. Christians who cultivate an appreciation for God's grace and who seek to apply that grace to every area of their lives, position themselves to know a joyfulness and effectiveness that only God can grant. For married Christians, no area of application could be more urgent than one's own marriage.

In this chapter we look at how the grace that justifies (declaring us holy in God's sight) becomes the grace that sanctifies (making us ever more holy in daily life). Though the same grace, they have different purposes. Sanctifying grace is not new grace, or a change in grace. It is grace—the same grace that saved us—applied to the new heart of the child of God, a heart changed by saving grace.

As we practice renouncing sin, sanctifying grace teaches us how to replace the passions of this world with godliness. As a result, we grow in charitable thoughts, patience with our spouse, self-control instead of angry words, love, joy, peace . . . a virtually unlimited array of godly motivations and actions that look increasingly like the character of Christ and combine to make marriage sweet.

Key Idea: *Sanctifying grace is good news. It's the news that God gives persistent grace to run the race.*

Robert Murray M'Cheyne closes this chapter by reminding us that "For one look at yourself, take ten looks at Christ." For this to happen, we need help. It's easy to have our spiritual perspective skewed by paying too much attention to what we see inside. How can we help one another along? Here are four things to keep in mind when encouraging your spouse in the grace of God.

1. Your spouse is inclined to drift from grace to self-effort.

2. Your spouse may tend to become discouraged.

3. Your spouse can lose sight of the ultimate goal.

4. Your spouse must be pointed not to grace alone, but to the one from whom all grace flows.

When a spouse communicates grace, we move beyond mistakes and the journey becomes enjoyable. That's the way it's supposed to be when sinners say "I do."

Grace—amazing, persistent grace—is helping us each day to run the race of renouncing, living, waiting, and wanting. The grace of God has appeared with a power so stubborn that it will not allow sin to ultimately win.

Gospel Application

For Me:

1. How have you seen grace at work helping you replace the passions of this world with godliness?

2. What are you aware of right now where you need "persistent grace to run the race" (p. 139)?

3. In what ways are you having to "wait" right now—to have confidence that God is at work in areas of your life that don't seem to change?

For Us:

1. Each of you communicate areas where you are personally tempted to discouragement and take some time to pray for each other—both immediately and in an ongoing way.

2. Each of you complete the sentence: Encouragement is really helpful to me when . . .

Gospel Interaction—
Small Group Discussion

1. If you have worked on the *Gospel Application* questions above, share some of your answers with your small group.

2. What did you learn in this chapter about grace that you didn't think about before?

3. Are there areas in your life where you are aware that God's grace is "coaching you" toward godliness? How are you experiencing the coaching of grace in the following areas:

   • Making effort to renounce sin that entangles you
   • Making positive changes to obey God

4. How well do you do encouraging your spouse? What is one thing from the discussion on pp. 146–149 that you can apply in your marriage to help each other against discouragement?

Responses:

Gospel Reflection

QUOTE: *"Human sin is stubborn, but not as stubborn as the grace of God and not half so persistent, not half so ready to suffer to win its way."*

—Cornelius Plantinga, p. 139

SCRIPTURE: TITUS 2:11–14

Notes:

Chapter Nine

Concerning Sex

Gospel Implication

*H*onest conversation about sex can be difficult. Open the door on the subject of intimacy and you can end up addressing topics ranging from the secret to the volatile, and from the embarrassing to the joyful. Yet the strengths and weaknesses of a marriage are often more obvious in the bedroom than anywhere else. If you really want your marriage to grow sweeter through the years, you have to examine the fine print about your sex life.

Reading 1 Corinthians leaves no doubt: God cares about sexuality—and he cares as much about its proper expression as he does its improper expression. We probably already know more than we need to about the second category. How about we focus on the first?

Key Idea: *Sex is an adventure in devotion, delight and dependence.*

Sex in marriage is an adventure in devotion. A biblical view of sexual intimacy means that we are devoted to protecting one another from sexual temptation beyond the marriage covenant. We are devoted to one another's rights as the Bible defines them—we are to seek the best interests of each other in sexual intimacy.

Sex in marriage is an adventure in delight. We are to see sex as a gift from God and a means of grace toward one another. It is not meant to be a duty performed, but an experience of growth and relationship in which we take delight throughout our lives.

Sex in marriage is an adventure in dependence. While it is a means of grace, sex also is an area in need of grace. All couples battle through some adversity for the sake of intimacy, whether that be situational or physical challenges, or challenges of the heart—like sloth, unbelief and bitterness.

Gospel Application

For Me:

1. Which of the following might be the greatest challenge you face in regard to sexual intimacy right now—sloth, unbelief, or bitterness? How can you begin to apply grace to overcome these personal hindrances?

2. What are some of the influences in your life that have shaped your view of romance and sex? How can you begin to weed their influence out of your life?

For Us:

Use the "Let's Talk" sections in this chapter (pp. 156, 158, 161) to talk about how to grow in your communication over sex in your marriage.

Gospel Interaction—
Small Group Discussion

This chapter may be best discussed as an assignment for couples and not covered as a group assignment.

1. If you have worked on the *Gospel Application* questions above, share some of your answers with your small group.

2. What, in this chapter, did you find new or unfamiliar? How did it affect your thinking?

3. What are some ways men and women can view the issue of romance differently? How can these differences negatively affect the intimacy of marriage?

4. What are some practical challenges you face as a couple (schedules, parenting, etc.) that you need to work around to build romance and intimacy in your marriage?

5. Describe your most romantic experience as a couple and what made it that way.

Responses:

Gospel Reflection

QUOTE: *"The reason there is so much misery in marriage is not that husbands and wives seek their own pleasure, but that they do not seek it in the pleasure of their spouses."*

—John Piper, p. 158

SCRIPTURE: HEBREWS 11:6

Notes:

Chapter Ten

When Sinners Say Goodbye

Gospel Implication

*S*cripture sets forth an unfashionable goal for believers: God wants us to die well. This has nothing to do with estate-planning. It speaks of whether, through sanctification, our souls are prepared for the inevitable reality of death. The youth-fixated, pain-averse, escapist nature of western culture is an anomaly in human history. Here, preparation for death seems morbid. But throughout history, and in most of the world today, death has always been part of life and deserving of attention. The Puritans, in their admirable "Let's bring God into every moment" perspective, saw marriage as not simply a great way to live, but as a training ground for what lay beyond. Pastor Richard Baxter saw one of the goals of marriage as this: "To prepare each other for the approach of death, and comfort each other in the hopes of life eternal." Does our view of marriage ignore this inevitability, or prepare for it?

Key Idea: *Marriage is not just for life, it is a preparation for the life to come.*

Every married person is united to a mate in decay. "Treasure in jars of clay" is what Paul call us (2 Cor. 4:7). It's an image that fits well, whether you are on the engagement side of the wedding or stacking up anniversaries by the decade. And caring for clay is part of the calling of marriage. We have the joy of preparing one another for heaven even as earth makes its claim on the body. We enjoy front-row seats to the inner renewal even as we see the container wasting away.

A maturing marriage is one that sees all the way to the finish line and beyond. As married Christians, God bestows upon us the extraordinary honor of nurturing and celebrating the inner renewal while also caring for the outer decay. It's an adventure in irony, made possible by the gospel, the only real treasure in our brittle jars of clay. Not every married Christian sees this clearly. But joy awaits those who do.

Matthew Henry once said, "It ought to be the business of every day to prepare for our last day." When we gaze upon the cross, we begin to see the early light of a glorious day. Your marriage now, my marriage now, prepares us for that day. Marriage exists to point us and others to that day. Our marriages here are an amazing but imperfect picture of what we are looking forward to enjoying in eternal relationship with our Savior.

Gospel Application

For Me:

1. What are your thoughts and feelings on death? How might they affect how you currently live your life?

2. Read the Spurgeon quote on heaven at the end of the chapter. How does this quote inspire your love for Christ?

For Us:

1. After reading this chapter, how do you think you might need to view your marriage differently to prepare for the later years?

2. Where will you be as a couple in ten years? What would you like your marriage to look like at that time?

Gospel Interaction—
Small Group Discussion

1. If you have worked on the *Gospel Application* questions above, share some of your answers with your small group.

2. Have you ever seen an elderly married couple that you admired? What about their marriage did you find attractive?

3. How did Mark and Carol's story affect you? What can you learn from it for where you live right now?

4. What can you learn from Jere's story for where you are right now?

5. In looking over the book, which chapter do you think you would most likely go back and read through again? Why?

Responses:

Gospel Reflection

Quote: "Heaven is always heaven, and unspeakably full of blessedness; but even heaven has its holidays, even bliss has its overflowings; [But] on that day when the springtide of the infinite ocean of joy shall have come, what a measureless flood of delight shall overflow the souls of all glorified spirits as they perceive that the consummation of love's great design is come— "The marriage of the Lamb is come, and his wife hath made herself ready"! We do not know yet, beloved, of what happiness we are capable . . . Oh, may I be there! . . . If I may but see the King in his beauty, in the fullness of his joy, when he shall take by the right hand her for whom he shed his precious blood, and shall know the joy which was set before him, for which he endured the cross, despising the shame, I shall be blest indeed! Oh, what a day that will be when every member of Christ shall be crowned in him, and with him, and every member of the mystical body shall be glorified in the glory of the Bridegroom! A day will come, the day of days, time's crown and glory, when . . . the saints, arrayed in the righteousness of Christ, shall be eternally one with him in living, loving, lasting union, partaking together of the same glory, the glory of the Most High. What must it be to be there!"

—C.H. Spurgeon, p. 182

Scripture: 2 Corinthians 4:16–17